Nathaniel Sands

The Philosophy of Teaching

The teacher, the pupil, the school

Nathaniel Sands

The Philosophy of Teaching
The teacher, the pupil, the school

ISBN/EAN: 9783337068509

Printed in Europe, USA, Canada, Australia, Japan

Cover: Foto ©Paul-Georg Meister /pixelio.de

More available books at **www.hansebooks.com**

The Philosophy of Teaching.

———〜〜〜———

THE TEACHER,

THE PUPIL, THE SCHOOL.

BY

NATHANIEL SANDS.

HARPER & BROTHERS, PUBLISHERS,

FRANKLIN SQUARE.

1869.

TEACHER AND PUPIL.

THE TEACHER, THE PUPIL, THE SCHOOL.

TEACHER AND PUPIL.

OF the various callings to which the division of labor has caused man specially to devote himself, there is none to be compared for nobility or usefulness with that of the true teacher. Yet neither teachers nor people at present realize this truth.

Among the very few lessons of value which might be derived from so-called "classical" studies, is that of the proper estimate in which the true teacher should be held; for among the Greeks no calling or occupation was more honored. Yet with a strange perversity, albeit for centuries the precious time of youth has been wasted, and the minds and morals of the young perverted by "classical" studies, this one lesson has been disregarded.

What duty can be more responsible, what vocation more holy, than that of training the young in habits of industry, truthfulness, economy, and sobriety; of giving to them that knowledge and skill without which their lives would become a burden to themselves and to society? Yet, while the merchant seeks to exercise the greatest caution in selecting the persons to whom he intrusts his merchandise, and yields respect to him who faithfully performs his commercial engagements, he makes but scant inquiry as to the character or qualifications of the MIND-BUILDER upon whose skill, judgment, and trustworthiness the future of his children will greatly depend.

The position assigned by our social rules to the teacher accords, not with the nobility of his functions, but with the insufficient appreciation entertained of them by the people, and is accompanied by a corresponding inadequate remuneration. And what is the result? Except a few single-hearted, noble men and women, by whom the profession of the teacher is illustrated and adorned ; except a few self-sacrificing heroes and heroines whose love of children and of mankind reconciles them to an humble lot and ill-requited labors, the class of school-teachers throughout the whole civilized world barely reaches the level of that mediocrity which in all other callings suffices to obtain not merely a comfortable maintenance in the present, but a provision against sickness and for old age.

What aspiring father, what Cornelia among mothers, select for their children the profession of a teacher as a field in which the talents and just ambition of such children may find scope? Nor can we hope for any improvement until a juster appreciation of the nobility of the teacher's vocation, and a more generous remuneration of his labors shall generally prevail.

It is to the desire to aid somewhat in bringing about a juster appreciation in the minds alike of teachers and of people of the utility and nobleness of the teacher's labors and vocation that these pages owe their origin.

When we consider the nature of the Being over whose future the teacher is to exercise so great an influence, whose mind he is to store with knowledge, and whom he is to train in the practice of such conduct as shall lead to his happiness and well-being, we are lost in amazement at the extent of the knowledge and perfection of the moral attributes which should have been acquired by the teacher. It is his duty to make his pupils acquainted with that nature of which they form a part, by which they are surrounded, and which is "rubbing against them at every step in life." But he can not teach that of which he himself is ignorant. Every science then may in turn become necessary or desirable to be employed as an instructive agent, every art may be made accessory to illustrate some item of knowledge or to elucidate some moral teaching.

Man is his subject, and with the nature of that subject and of his surroundings he must be acquainted, that the object to be attained and the means for its attainment may be known to him.

What is man? What are his powers, what is his destiny, and for what purpose and for what object was he created? Let us enter the laboratory of the chemist and commence our labors. Let us take down the crucible and begin the analysis, and endeavor to solve this important problem. In studying the great Cosmos we perceive each being seeking its happiness according to the instincts implanted in him by the Creator, and only in man we see his happiness made dependent on the extent to which he contributes to the happiness of others. What, so far as we can see, would this earth be without any inhabitants? What great purpose in the economy of nature could it serve? A palace without a king, a house without an occupant, a lonely and tenantless world, while we now see it framed in all its beauty for the enjoyment of happiness.

The Being upon whom the art and science of the teacher is to be exercised is one to whom food, clothing, fuel, and shelter are needful; possessed of organs of digestion, whose functions should be made familiar to their possessor; of breathing organs, to whose healthful exercise pure air is essential; a being full of life and animation, locomotive—desirous of moving from place to place; an emotional being, susceptible to emotions of joy and sorrow, love and hate, hope and fear, reverence and contempt, and whose emotions should be so directed that their exercise should be productive of happiness to others. He is also an intellectual being, provided with senses by which to receive impressions and acquire a knowledge of external things; with organs of comparison and of reason, by which to render available for future use the impressions received through the senses in the past. Lastly: he is also a social being, to whom perpetual solitude would be intolerable; sympathizing in the pains and pleasures of others, needing their protection, sympathy and co-operation for his own comfort, and desirous of conferring protection upon and of co-operating with them. But, further, he is a being who desires to be loved and esteemed, and finds the greatest charm of existence in the love and esteem he receives; to be loved and esteemed and cared for, he must love, esteem and care for others, and be generally amiable and useful.

Such is the Being, susceptible of pain and pleasure, of sorrow and joy, whom the MIND-BUILDER is to train up so that, as far as possible, the former may be averted and the latter secured.

The teacher, then, must train him in habits of industry and skill, that work may be pleasant and easy to him, and held in honorable esteem; for without work, skillfully performed, neither food, clothing, fuel nor shelter can be obtained in sufficient quantity to avoid poverty and suffering. Knowledge also must be acquired by the laborer, in order that the work which is to be skillfully performed may be performed with that attention to the conditions of mechanical, chemical, electrical, and vital agencies necessary to render labor productive. A knowledge of the conditions of mechanics, of chemistry, of electricity, and of vital phenomena should be imparted by the teacher; and to impart this knowledge, he must first possess it.

How sublime, then, are the qualifications, natural and acquired, which the true teacher should possess! How deep should be our reverence for him who, by his skill and knowledge, is capable, and by his moral qualities willing, to perform duties so onerous and so difficult. What station in life can be regarded as more exalted; whose utility can be compared with that of him who proves himself faithful to the duties he assumes, when he takes upon himself the office of a teacher of youth?

The question which is ever present to the mind of the true teacher is: What can I do to insure the happiness of these beings confided to my charge, whose minds it is given to me to fashion, not according to my will, but according as my skill and judgment shall, more or less, enable me to adapt my teachings to their natures? What shall I seek to engrave upon the clear tablets of their young and tender minds, in order that their future lot may be a joyous one? Let me illustrate (he will say) my profession. I will raise it high as the most honored among men, and for my monument I will say: "Look around; see the good works of those whom I have taught and trained; they are my memorials!"

Such may, such will become the hope and aspiration common to teachers in that good day to come, when their labors shall be honored as they deserve; when parents, in all the different ranks into which society falls, shall vie with each other in the respect and honor tendered to the teacher, whose true place in society is at least not beneath that of the Judge.

The teachers to be developed by such a state of society will, as their first step, seek to obtain a clear and comprehensive view of the work they propose to accomplish, and will then seek to adopt the most judicious means to reach the end proposed. They will adapt their methods of teaching to the nature of the object to be taught and to the order in which the faculties of the human mind naturally unfold themselves, for true education is the natural unfolding of the intellectual germ. In order to obtain the knowledge necessary of the object to be taught, the true teacher turns to nature as his guide, for the voice of nature is the voice of God, and in reading her statutes we read that grand volume in which He has left an impress of Himself. The science of nature is nothing more than the ability to read and interpret correctly the lessons taught. There was a period when mankind knew very little of the planet upon which they lived and moved and had their being; *there was a time when they knew almost nothing*; and there *will* come a time when they will know almost every thing that can be known by finite man. The earth is our *mother*, and *nature* is our teacher, and if we listen to her voice, she will lead us higher and higher until we will stand the master and the king in the glorified temple of wisdom. To reach results so grand and a position so exalted, our natures must unfold in exact harmony with all the laws' and forces which surround and control us from the time our existence commences until its close.

From the period of conception until birth the child draws to itself all the essential elements required for the organization of a human being; the capabilities and powers of the parent are taxed and called upon to contribute their material to enable nature to reproduce itself.

The child is born, and then, in a higher and more enlarged and more independent state of existence, commences drawing to itself the materials and substances necessary for its growth and unfolding. It draws in its mother's milk, it draws in the air, and it builds up in itself the unseen forces of life. Nature, true to her mission, goes on unfolding the child, and teaches it daily and hourly the lessons best adapted to its condition. In a few days after it is born, its powers of observation begin to show signs of life and action, and it can distinguish light from darkness; in a few weeks its mother and nurse are known—in a few months quickened intelligence displays itself in all its actions; in about twelve months it has learned the most difficult art of balancing itself so as to walk,, and also to speak a few words; at from two to two and a half years of age, only thirty months from birth, it has learned a language which it speaks, and has become familiar with a vast number of things surrounding it. From a state of entire ignorance it has in thirty months learned what would fill volumes. Horses, cows, pigs, dogs, toys, whips, birds, people, trees, houses, fruit, food, clothes, music, sounds, parents, friends, and a thousand other things are all familiar to it. Without professional teachers, almost without effort, all this valuable and indispensable knowledge has been acquired, through the unconscious adoption on the part of the mother of the true system of education—*e duco*—I lead forth, and hence nurse, cherish, build up, develop.

The child feels or reaches out, like the tendril, to the material world, seeking to make itself acquainted with that world; even the young infant soon begins to observe closely, soon knows its mother from all other persons, clings to her, loves her above all; soon it recognizes light from darkness, sweet from bitter; soon, when it sees a dog it will recognize it and jump with delight almost out of its mother's arms; it will show an eager delight to watch the motions of the horse, and imitates the sounds employed by adults when driving. He spreads forth the tentacles of his feeble mind for knowledge, and his mind "grows by what it feeds upon," and it is for those intrusted with the infant's training to respond intelligently to the child's desire, to place within its reach the mental food adapted to its digestion, to nourish and develop it so that its mental hunger shall be at once gratified and excited anew.

It is here, and to this end, that the able teacher steps in, to perfect the development of the future man and woman. He educates, by assisting the natural unfolding of the intellectual germ, he places within reach of the child-mind the food needed to its growth, and the child-mind reaches out its tentacles and absorbs the nourishment offered to it. Thus the mind grows from *within outward*, and the teacher aids its development, as the careful husbandman by tilling and enriching the soil according to the nature of the plant he cultivates, produces a healthy and fruitful plant.

The true teacher does not seek to teach by simply putting books into the child's hand, and bidding it to learn; he addresses himself to those faculties and powers of the child's mind, which bring it in relation with the world in which it lives. Sight, hearing, touch, smell, taste, and thence observation, judgment, perception, reason, memory, hope, imagination, and the love of the beautiful are appealed to, developed and strengthened by natural exercise, even as the organs and limbs of the body are developed and strengthened by gymnastic and other appropriate exercises.

Education, mental and physical, is but the ABSORPTION of surrounding elements into the mind and body—an arrangement an assimilation of materials so as to incorporate them into the being to whose nourishment they are applied, just as the tree or plant assimilates to its growth and subsistence the materials which it draws from the air and the soil.

It is thus apparent that a great change in the system and principles now adopted in teaching is required, and if we change the principles we must, of course, change the instruments. These are now adapted to the method of teaching from WITHOUT inward. If we are to invert the system, and teach from within outward, then must our means and appliances be adapted to this change. The task, the forcing process, the stuffing and cramming must all give way to the natural mental growth, fostered, cherished, unfolded by culture, in accord with nature and with law. The inquiry then arises: What are to be the new means and appliances for mental culture? We have but to turn again to Nature as our teacher and our guide; her instincts are unerring. The seed germinates and pushes forth its root from within outward. The expansion or growth takes place by means of the elements which it attracts to itself, when these are placed within its reach, and towards which it stretches forth its organs. These elements it assimilates into and makes a part of itself. This process of Nature, so familiar to most of us, serves to illustrate exactly what should take place in intellectual growth. The mind hungers and feels out for and is impelled by a natural internal impulse to gather to itself the elements of knowledge; the wise teacher steps forward and becomes to the germinating intellect what the sun and dew and rain are to the plant. The mind must be fed in conformity with its longings, its wants, its desires. "Blessed are they that hunger and thirst after righteousness."

The teacher develops this hunger and thirst by stimulating inquiry, and by presenting to the mind the use and beauty of knowledge; and when the mind gives signs that its hunger is temporarily appeased, that time is now required for mental digestion and assimilation, the wise teacher rests, and would no more attempt to stuff and cram the mind than the wise mother would seek to force food into her child's stomach.

Intellectual growth of some kind, not less than bodily growth, whether good or evil, is constantly taking place. It should be the teacher's care to render that growth a healthy one, calculated to insure the happiness of the subject, and, in securing his own happiness, to contribute to the happiness of others.

The body being visible to the physical eye, its growth is also visible, and we do not think of feeling impatient at the long months and years required for it to attain its full proportions; nor do we seek by any forcing process to produce a man at 10 instead of at 20 or 30 years of age.

Were the mind and its growth also visible to the eye, we would be equally careful in our treatment of it. Man's first impulse in an uncivilized state has generally been a resort to force for the accomplishment of his objects; and as he took his first step forward the habits of his barbaric life remained with him. Hence, the first steps in teaching were by force—the lash, the rod, the school penal code; but even as when hungry, wholesome and well-dressed food rejoices us, so will the mind gladly accept the mental food carefully prepared for it by the true teacher.

We live in a world adapted by its Creator to our happiness and highest well-being. It is not only possible, but casy, to win from Nature all that is necessary or desirable, for our sustenance and comfort. It is the true teacher's duty to fit the child thus to win its happiness; and such a teacher has ever present to his mind the question: How am I to perform this duty? What sort of teaching and training am I to give to the subjects of my care? Let us endeavor to find some direction to guide us to Nature's answer to this question.

TEACHING AND TRAINING.

2

WHETHER we regard private schools or public schools, boarding or day schools, we find that much which goes on at them affords an important lesson, not as to what to follow, but what to avoid.

Is there any thing worthy of the name, of confiding intercourse between teacher and pupil known upon this continent, or to extend our inquiry, we may say, known anywhere? Here and there exceptional instances will be found, as we have before said, both in this country and in Europe, of men and women devoted to their noble profession, between whom and their pupils there has grown up the strongest bond of parental and fraternal affection. To these teachers the pupils run in every difficulty for its solution, in every danger for protection; but with these exceptions the teacher is looked upon as a task-master, sometimes even as a spy; the tasks set to be shirked as much as possible, the observation of the teacher to be eluded and deceived.

Lesson-time over, the children resort to their tame animals, to their weaving-machines, their wind-mills and dams; to their gardens, kites and ships; to swimming, rowing, foot-ball, marbles, leap-frog, base-ball and cricket. In the practice of these games, skill, dexterity and knowledge are acquired of which the pupils appreciate the utility, and enjoy not only for present, but for anticipated future use.

Natural History, to be taught in school and made a reality, by following the guide given us by nature in the amusements to which children resort of their own accord, should be a prominent subject of instruction and training in the school. Cultivating the faculties of observation and of analysis, it should be among the earliest subjects of instruction, and, at the same time, of amusement.

But they ought not to be taught from books; nature and the teacher are the only books to be employed until considerable progress has been made by the pupils. It is so easy to procure the things themselves for the study of botany; an abundant supply of wild flowers can be so readily obtained, sufficient to enable each child to be supplied with specimens for examination and dissection. The interest of the children in their study can be so easily awakened and sustained by the judicious teacher, the difficulties of the supposed hard words of scientific names disappear so readily, that the real difficulty is to understand how so obvious a subject of instruction is either wholly banished from the schools, or sought to be taught only from books, without any reference to living nature.

The variety and multiplicity of insect life affords ample opportunity for the study of that branch of natural history—and entomology would be found not less beautiful and interesting than botany; the delightful excursions in which teachers and pupils would join for the gathering of objects of natural his-

tory would at the same time serve to strengthen the
bond of affection which should exist between them.
The nature of his own body and the functions of his
various organs will soon interest the pupil, and along
with instruction therein he would learn the qualities
of the different kinds of animal and vegetable substances in use for food, their relative value and importance in building up his body; he would learn to
compare the food now in use with that which was
employed by our ancestors, and what has given rise
to the adoption of the new and abandonment of the
old; the methods of cookery best adapted to each
kind of food, and what kinds of food are suitable for
particular ages and states of health; what material,
vegetable or animal, is most suitable for clothing, sep-
arately or in combination. He would learn to compare our present style of clothing with that adopted
in past ages; he would learn the history of the
changes which have been adopted, and while feeling
desirous of retaining such as have been wisely adopted, might learn from past experience to desire to return to some good habits as to clothing which have
been abandoned.

The tight-fitting garments in which we unhealthi-
ly clothe our bodies, a fashion for which we are in-
debted to the use of armor in times when the chief
occupation of man was mutual slaughter, and the
great object of desire to secure protection against hos-
tile weapons, might some time come to be discarded
for the more healthful practices of the ancient Asiat-
ics and Romans, if a general knowledge of the un-
healthfulness of our present practices should come to
prevail.

The necessity and meaning of light and cleanliness, the indifference of the human body to all natural changes of temperature, when strengthened and maintained in health by·wholesome food and efficient bathing, might lead to the taking of effective measures to restore the old Roman bath to general use.

As regards shelter, why a building on the ground is generally to be preferred to a cave or shelter in the ground—what materials are best adapted for roofs, what for walls, floors, windows, why we use stone or brick in one part of the country and wood in another; what sizes, shapes, means of warmth and ventilation, for privacy and social enjoyment, should be adopted, and as regards furniture and utensils, what are most suitable for the several parts of a dwelling; what should guide our selection of material, fabrics, shape, size and pattern; how to establish a communication from one part of a building to another; how water and light are to be had most readily. All these things should form the subject of school study and inquiry.

The means of locomotion, how streets, roads and paths should be laid out and maintained; the construction and use of carriages, cars, wagons, tramways, railroads, ships, steamers, propelling power; where bridges should be built, and how; viaducts and embankments to cross valleys, cuttings and tunnels to penetrate hills and mountains; these, too, simply at first, and afterwards in more elaborate detail, should form subjects of school instruction, the rules determining the selection of each and the methods of their construction not being preached in lectures, *ex Cathedra*, but evolved by a patient questioning of nature, by experiment and the Socratic method of inquiry. Exercise of the limbs under the direction of a skilled instructor, so that all the muscles of the body may be duly trained, and a healthy body built up to support a healthy mind. The kinds of recreation to be selected, whether bull-baiting, cock-fighting, rat-catching or prize-fighting, should be preferred to games of skill and strength, to the drama, literature, works of art, public walks, gardens, and museums; the comparative influence of all these upon the health, strength, courage, activity, humanity, refinement and happiness of society; how people may be led to prefer such as tend to general well-being to those which have a tendency to brutalize and debase. ' All these also should be dwelt upon in the school.

How stores of food, of clothing, of fuel and of the materials for building may be collected, and preserved; how present labor may be made to supply future wants, and the thought of future enjoyment be made to sweeten the present toil.. How the means of instruction and of amusement may be secured. How all engaged in supplying one need of society co-operate with all who are engaged in supplying its other needs. What form of government is best, and how it may be best administered. How upright judges may be secured, justice administered, and society protected against internal and external foes. These and all the other subjects enumerated would, if handled by a true teacher, be found most attractive to children.

The names given to the subjects at which we have glanced are: Natural History, the Mathematical and Physical Sciences in all their branches, Vegetable and

Animal Physiology, the Political and Social Sciences; which should be presented in the order in which the attention and desire to learn could be aroused.

It will hardly fail to strike the mind of the reader that nothing has yet been said about giving instruction in the use of those tools for acquiring knowledge, reading, writing, ciphering and drawing. The true teacher will understand the omission. The commencement of the instruction in reading, writing, ciphering, drawing, and in spelling, would take place as part of the object lesson which should be adopted as the first step to knowledge, and should be retained in the most advanced classes as the most perfect method of applying the knowledge which has been acquired. It would soon be understood by the pupils that the power of reading, of writing, of designing and of calculating is essential to the acquirement of knowledge, and to any thing like extent and variety of information on subjects relating to individual and social well-being. The desire of acquiring this knowledge would quicken the faculties of the children, augment their industry, and lighten the labors of the teacher to an indefinable extent. The teacher who should fail to impart a moderate degree of skill in these arts to most, and of excellence to many, at the same time that adequate progress was made in the study of the sciences we have named, should be deemed unfit for his profession, and not be allowed to relieve himself from disgrace by magnifying the difficulties of his task or by complaints of the idleness or want of capacity of his pupils. As children will take interest in what they learn in proportion to their understanding of its bearing upon their own happiness, and upon their actual life and surroundings, the knowledge of themselves as beings acted upon by surrounding objects and by their own kind, should be carefully imparted to them simultaneously with the knowledge of the qualities of the surrounding objects destined to act upon them.

Children thus worked upon by skilled and earnest instructors; led to find out and observe the properties of that Nature of which they form a part; their minds nourished by the enjoyment which follows the mastering of every difficulty, and the addition of every fresh item of knowledge to their previous store; trained also in habits of healthfulness and of amiability: will not only cheerfully give themselves to study, but will also seek to dignify by their conduct and to improve by practice the knowledge they progressively acquire, soon understanding, among other things, why they are sent to school and the importance of that education, part of which they are to acquire at school.

As the object of the school-teaching should be to prepare the pupils for actual life, they should be made familiar with the idea that all their means of subsistence and enjoyment can only be obtained by labor; not only should their attention be called to the fact, but they should be made sensible how much skill, knowledge and labor and economy were needed for the creation of existing stores, and are needed for their maintenance in undiminished quantity; nor can this be done in any way more fitly or completely than by performing under their eyes, and causing them to take part in, the actual business of production. The well-ordered school is an industrial school, in which every industrial occupation, manufacturing

or agricultural, for the carrying on of which conven-
ience can be made, should be successively practised by
the children, under the direction of skilled workers.

The farm, the factory, the shop, the counting-house
and the kitchen, should each have its type in the
school, and present to the minds of the children a picture of real life; while their practice would impart a
skill and adaptability to the pupils which would insure their preparedness for all the vicissitudes of the
most eventful life.

Can any reason be suggested for adopting a different system of instruction for girls than that which
shall be determined on as best fitted for boys? We
confess to our inability to perceive any—both are or-
ganisms of the same all-pervading nature—to both
the most intimate knowledge of that which skill and
perseverance secure, seems to be desirable for their
happiness, and that of all mankind. Of the two, perhaps, the greatest knowledge is needed for the woman, FOR HERS IS THE MORE IMPORTANT AND MORE
PERFECTED ORGANISM; to her is committed the per-
formance of the chief functions of the highest act of
organized beings, viz., reproduction; therefore, upon
her knowledge and conduct, far more than upon that
of the man, depends the future of the beings in whom
she is to live again.

Another great object with the true teacher, will be
so to train the judgment of his pupils as to avoid that
forming of unconsidered opinion which is the parent
of prejudice and a chief obstacle to progress. Trained to investigate the foundations of every fact in nature and in science, to weigh the evidences on which
they are asked to receive assertions, whether of a

physical, moral or social nature, they will ever have
a reason for the faith that is in them ; and will know
how to SUSPEND JUDGMENT when the means of knowledge are insufficient.

Such pupils will not be apt to form opinions either
in physical science, politics, or industrial life, without
having first thoroughly examined the bases of the
opinions they form and express, while the prejudices imbibed from nurses or parents, will be subject-
ed to vigorous investigation, and either received as
sound doctrine, or discarded as ill-founded and superstitious.   Of how many prejudices are we not the
victims, without being ourselves in the least conscious of the fact!   Our political opinions, our social
customs, are taken up like the fashion of a coat, without reason or reflection ; and habit and association,
but too often hold us captive long after reason has
pronounced her condemnation ; our minds have been
warped from truth, and we fail to perceive our own
deficiency, to recognize the mental dishonesty with
which we are afflicted.   All this will be averted in
the case of those who in their youth are trained to a
rigorous investigation of every fact presented to their
minds, until the habit of truth, not merely of speaking and telling the truth, but that mental truthfulness
which shrinks from accepting a falsehood for truth,
and acknowledges ignorance rather than utter what
is not assured—will become as much a part of the
pupil's nature as is his desire for food.   In short, he
would be so trained as to feel as great a repugnance
to plunge his mind into moral, as his body into material filth.

Again, while ever merciful and pitying to the

criminal, he would be intolerant of falsehood wherever
it might be found; and he would deem himself der-
elict in his duty, as a man and as a citizen, did he
leave corruption to rot and fester in the Common-
wealth, because he and others like him would not
take the trouble to raise their voices against wrong-
doers!

What a different aspect would not this great city
of New York offer to our inspection to what it now
presents, had a generation been trained in the knowledge, and practised in the observance of their duties
as citizens!

Did those merchants and traders, who, in their
private dealings would scorn a lie, but recognize the
duty they owe as citizens and as men of truth, they
would, by uniting, soon sweep away the serious dis-
credit to our country and to Republican Institutions,
the festering corruption of this city and of the State;
yet it is to their supine, nay wicked tolerance of the
evil that we owe the specimens of judicial corruption
by which we are robbed and dishonored. Can it be
said that any system of education can be sound,
which shall fail to demonstrate, at least to the older
pupils, their duties as citizens, to take an active, intel-
ligent and upright interest in public affairs; that
shall fail to instruct them in the principles by which
their judgments should be guided, and lead them to
discard every action in public affairs, which they
would not approve in private life?

We must cease to live in books, in past mystifica-
tions, in useless theories, in foolish and unprofitable
discussions, in ancient ideas and customs, and grasp
the living present with all the richness, fullness and

beauty of its life. The chemistry of nature, the work of her great laboratory, should be the study of youth as of age, instead of dead languages and the vain and foolish mythology of Greeks and Romans wherewith at present we poison the minds of the young.

"Can we take burning coals into our bosom and not be burned?" Can we suffer the impressionable minds of youth to be impregnated with the filth of the heathen poets in their imaginings of gods as disgusting as themselves, without staining the pure tablet of the mind with spots and grossness, while the children acquire a distaste for that glorious nature whose volume should be their constant study?

We have to deal with the great present, with life, not with death—to promote health, physical and moral, not to propagate infectious sickness. The present, wisely improved, leads to a happy future, and is the only road to that goal. We can not jump the present and its duties and reach the future so as to enjoy it, neither can the dead past lighten the labors of the living present. There is a past which still lives and vivifies the present, but the quaint and filthy imagery in which the ancient priests disguised from the profane—from all but the initiated—the mysteries of their lore, can be of small account to a people whose great duty is the dissemination of light and truth.

Every thing that has any relation to man's comfort and well-being, or to his happiness as a social being, that it is, and not the dead past that we should learn, and of the things that affect us most nearly we should learn first. What did the ancients know of steam, of electricity, of the material elements of nature, of her forces? And little as we know, how much of that little could be learned from a lifelong study of ancient lore? If there be aught of value in the laws of ancient Rome which has not been translated into our native tongue, let it be translated; but let not our youth waste precious years in learning to play upon an instrument (Greek or Latin) which when learned can give forth no sound. But if we turn to Nature and to her grand volume, we there find all the knowledge man can acquire. From her study, too, we can learn a lesson, not perhaps among the least important, as to the limits fixed by nature to human knowledge. To know of a surety what those things are which never can be known to mortal man, is a knowledge, the want of which has driven many to puerile and superstitious practices, and many more to madness and despair.

From the great book of Nature, God's book, is to be learned the principle of justice, of love, of wisdom, of truth; and as the germ of justice is developed in the mind, the mind is brought in contact with the Great Fountain, absorbs a portion of its light, enlarges, develops, becomes stronger, assimilates to itself the essence of the great Godhead, and renders man godlike.

So with each of the other faculties of man; each draws its nourishment from its special FOUNTAIN. Wisdom, love, justice, and truth should preside; and if judgment, sympathy and conscientiousness be judiciously trained and developed, they will help to develop harmoniously all the other faculties. But to this end they, and each and all of man's faculties, must be brought into a wholesome, natural contact, each with its proper food; and by natural we mean

not that contact which might peradventure happen if
left uncared for, but such as the nature of the faculty
demands for its development in due harmony, to produce the greatest amount of happiness to its possessor.
To supply this food, to bring to each faculty its proper aliment, is the business of the true teacher. If we
desire a child to be truthful, we must bring it in contact with truth, and bring it to love truth by causing
its practice to inure to the child's enjoyment. If we
wish it to be wise, we must bring its mind in contact
with wisdom, exercise its analytical powers, and train
its judgment; let it see sound judgment producing
happiness; let it see how beautiful and desirable is
the possession of wisdom, and the child will soon
learn to seek it for its own sake.

To chastise a child for speaking that which is un-
true may fill it with fear, but does not make it love
truth. The love of truth and of wisdom must be cultivated as we cultivate the love of music. "Seek me
early, and ye shall find me." "Knock, and it shall
be opened unto you." That which the mind seeks it
will find. The natural relationships are established,
and it is only for us to work in harmony with, and
not obstruct or interfere with them. It is the "true
relationship of things" we need to learn. There is
nothing in us that is not in nature. All the forces
developed in man are but developments of nature;
and all the forces required for his nourishment and
strength exist in the bosom of Nature. Matter,
light, heat, electricity are not produced by him. In
nature they exist; remove any one of them and he
perishes. To Nature then must we ever turn as the
reservoir of nourishment and as the teacher, by the

study of whose volume we learn all of wisdom that can be known of mortal man, or that can tend to his well-being; and her true relationships must be the constant object of our search.   Before the knowledge of her true relationships disappear superstition and fear and mystery.   The lightning's flash, the thunder's roar, the falling meteor and the sun's eclipse cease to terrify and alarm.   Witches, hobgoblins and demons come no longer to trouble us; the most unusual phenomena awaken only philosophical research and curiosity.   And what is true of the full-grown man is not less true of the child.

That school wherein children above the age of infancy fail to assist the teacher in his instruction, is an ill-ordered school.   It is not the subject, but the teacher who is uninteresting; he scolds, worries and punishes his pupils, when he himself is the fitter subject for the lash.   He awakens the sense of fear which should lie dormant, while the other faculties of his pupils slumber in spiritless inactivity.

As the object of education is to prepare children to enter successfully and happily into life, and wisely to discharge all the duties devolving upon them as they unfold into men and women, and occupy the sphere assigned to them, the simple rule for the course of instruction seems to be, that they should learn those things in the order in which they can be received by the child's mind, which most vitally affect their well-being and happiness.

As only a healthy, well-developed body can afford a home to a healthy, well-developed mind, physical culture claims early and constant attention, and should receive that careful regard to which the truth contained in the well-known aphorism: "We are fearfully and wonderfully made," entitles it. The teachings of the sciences of Pathology and of sanitary science should be judiciously and carefully elucidated, practically and theoretically; presented step by step to the mind of the child; and the child's body and mind should be carefully trained, so as to develop all its physical and mental powers in harmony. Gymnasiums for the body, conducted by men who have made themselves masters of anatomy and physiology, should be an essential feature in every school, so that ignorance and the desire to excel may not lead to putting a strain upon the system calculated materially to injure organs which need careful and judicious development. Plays, games, dancing, marching and the gymnasium all require the careful supervision of a teacher well versed in a practical knowledge of the human system, and thoroughly appreciative of the great truth, "We are fearfully and wonderfully made." But the foundation for the school as for the life career must be laid at home, and much as the teacher can do, he can never supply deficiencies resulting from the want of a well-ordered home or of a healthy home training. Never, save under necessity, should the parent yield up his sacred duty to another, at least during the tender years of childhood.

The education of the heart and of the affections, is as essential as the school education, and these can never be so well cultivated as under the influence of home. All must be developed in order to maintain the true equilibrium. The boarding-school is not the place for children to attain a sound moral devel-

opment, and the sooner parents generally understand
this truth, the better for their children, for themselves and for society. As well uproot the flower,
or shrub or tree, and expect it to flourish, as to cut
the child off from the influence of home, and the care
of a loving mother, father, brother and sister, and
hope that the sympathetic faculties of its mind can
attain their just development.

Physical culture, heretofore neglected among us—
the body being left to grow up as it may happen or
chance—will form a prominent feature of training in
every well-ordered school. All the muscles of the
body will be in turn exercised, developed. The ancient Greeks afforded us here also a wise example,
which we have signally failed to imitate.

Let us secure for our children all the advantages
we can from an enlightened and natural system of
education, and do all we can to perfect both mind
and body. How often is the cry repeated, "Mamma,
tell me a story," and mamma, tired and weary, says
she is too busy, or, for the want of a better, tells over
again for the hundredth time, "Little Red Riding
Hood," or some other equally foolish or more injurious tale, such as Bluebeard or Cinderella. An-
ecdotes of great men, suitably arranged, events in
history and biography, carrying with them valuable
and important morals, will afford all the amusement
the child desires, without developing a love for the
marvellous and false, which leads it away in infancy
from the simple, truthful, and natural. If children
are to be taught to think naturally and truthfully, we
can not begin too young, and it is the duty of parents to remember that Valentine and Orson, Cinder-

ella, Bluebeard, and such stories, are a web of false
and exaggerated statements that will, and do produce injurious effects upon the child's mind. The
story of Aladdin's Lamp has made many a child desire to enjoy wealth without labor, and has exerted a
most pernicious, though unsuspected, influence upon
his future. Children, not less than men, seek an easy
road to the objects of their desires; and while works
of imagination are to be by no means discarded in
mental training, such should not be selected as give
false notions of the busy and industrial life into
which the child is to be introduced. Even in the
choice and use of the finest works of fiction, the
greatest caution is necessary. The little one can
hardly distinguish between a fable that amuses it,
and a lie told to shield it from punishment. If it
hear nothing but truth, it will know nothing but
truth; and a truthful mind is a glorious thing to be-
hold in children as in men. "An idle brain is the
devil's workshop;" therefore let there be no idle
brains, but let all work usefully and pleasantly.
Usefully we say, for even amusement is useful. We
live in a world of use, in a world of beauty, a world
that can be greatly improved, and human happiness
largely increased, according as we avail ourselves of
the knowledge already acquired for the right teaching and training of the young, so that they may
grow up and develop into happy, self-supporting
men and women, diffusing happiness to all around,
themselves happy in proportion to the happiness
they cause.

THE SCHOOL.

UPON the organization and arrangement of the school largely depends the success of the educator. Two things must be borne constantly in mind. First, to create truthful and intellectual atmosphere, where wisdom, honor, and knowledge can 'be inhaled as with the breath, and second, to make the school cheerful and attractive in every way possible. We must get rid of the idea now generally prevailing among children, that the school is to be resorted to with regret and escaped from with pleasure.

So soon as the child will look at and become interested in pictures and toys, and will listen to tales and little stories, it can profitably be introduced in the school, the first department of which should be the Infant-school, or, as the Germans so aptly term it, the children's garden, or Kinder Garten.

Here plaiting, modelling, and building, with simple object lessons for the older infants, develop their powers of observation, and give employment and impart skill to little fingers which might else be engaged in destroying furniture or clothes, or in pilfering from the sugar-bowl. Practical familiarity with the properties of lines, angles, circles, spheres, cylinders, cubes, cones, and the conic sections will be acquired, which

will give a life and reality to the geometrical studies which will occupy them in their school career.
Dancing and singing will relieve the tedium of sitting, shake off the surplus energy, give rest to the
body, and power, time, and tune to the voice. Mod-
els of houses, stores, workshops, kitchens, farms, and
factories, which later on they will assist in making,
will be a source alike of amusement and instruction.

In the children's garden no teacher should have
charge of more than about twelve children, who
should regard her as their mother-teacher, while she
should seek to win the love and confidence of the little ones as the beginning of her work.

Each class of twelve should have their own special
room, while for general purposes, such as music, drilling, gymnastic exercises, games, tableaux, and exhi-
bitions of the magic lantern, the oxyhydrogen micro-
scope, the stereopticon, and the like, they should as-
semble in a large hall. The details of arrangements
will readily suggest themselves. The main feature is
to have all things natural, free, pleasant, cheerful,
bright, refined, and unrestrained by external forms or
rigid rules, at the same time that order is secured by
an easy discipline.

So deeply are we impressed with the importance
and utility of the kinder garten, and with the high
qualities required by the teacher of the very young,
that we are more and more disposed to believe that
the true order in rank and promotion among teachers should be, to speak in paradox, downwards; that
is to say, the younger the children to be taught, the
higher the rank and remuneration of the teacher; for
not only is an extensive range of knowledge neces-

sary to enable the teacher truthfully to answer the innumerable questions of inquisitive infancy, and to avoid giving false notions, to be afterwards with greater or less difficulty removed—always with a shock to the moral sentiment when the child discovers it has been deceived—but also a knowledge of the infant mind, a perception of the thoughts and fancies which chase one another through the infant brain, a knowledge and perceptive power which only a watchful and loving experience can acquire. An industry and a patience far beyond any needed by the teacher of more advanced pupils are also required by the highly-cultivated men and women, to whom alone the training of infant minds should be intrusted. Advanced pupils go more than half-way to meet their teacher—the infant can render no assistance to his, all has to be borne, suffered and done for him—his future habits depend mainly on those given to him in his earliest years. Yet the care of him in these important days is generally confided to ignorant nurses and to the less-skilled class of teachers.

In building the school, a pleasing style of architecture should be adopted, and the walls of the main hall should be hung with diagrams of all kinds, illustrative of natural history in its largest sense, of the sciences and of the mechanical arts, and with portraits or busts of distinguished men. The walls of the class-rooms should be decorated with diagrams and maps and figures referring to the special branches taught therein.

A large and commodious laboratory should be fitted up in the building, to enable every pupil to acquire experimentally that knowledge of chemical forces and action which books alone can never im-

part. A convenient observatory should afford facili-
ty for astronomical study and observation.

On the top floors or around the building should
be arranged workshops, where the use of tools and
machinery could be taught. . The classes should as-
semble in the large hall, in the morning, where they
might join in singing or light gymnastic exercises, or
listen to some short appropriate address before betak-
ing themselves to their class-rooms.

The teaching in these latter should be conducted,
wherever practicable, upon the Socratic method, and
every branch of science and of art could be thus ex-
plained. The mother unconsciously uses this method
in educating or drawing out the first perceptions of
infancy and early youth; and the impressions derived
from this method of acquiring knowledge are the most
lasting, being such as become most absolutely assimi-
lated with the pupil's mind. The teacher would also,
at frequent intervals, conduct his class into the fields
and woods for the study of botany, entomology, and
geology, where Nature would supply in abundance
the materials, and the teacher would be the only book.
Instruction in the various trades which could be con-
veniently practised should receive attention, the taste
of the pupils being made a guide to selection.

Some portion of the teaching which goes on in
school should be performed by the pupils, under the
supervision of the teacher. No adult can so thoroughly enter into a child's mind as can another child; nor
is this the only reason.

That is not fully known which can not be thoroughly used and applied, and knowledge can not be
applied which its possessor can not himself impart.

A perfect illustration of this truth is furnished us in the training of the soldier.

Upon nothing, perhaps, have the knowledge and skill of the most powerful intellects been more concentrated than upon the science and art of mutual slaughter; and in establishing the soldiers' drill, an exhaustive analysis of the means by which the desired object was to be attained has been pursued. The men whose intellects have developed that drill, have not been content to treat the soldier as a pupil only. Each recruit has in turn to teach, as well as to learn to practise what he has learned, by drilling others whom he is made temporarily to command, as well as to practise his drill under the command of his officer; for only by such means could the highest degree of efficiency be secured. The reasons which led to the adoption of this principle in the barrack apply equally to the school.

This principle of giving and receiving we also see exemplified in Nature. Animals inhale oxygen from the air and return carbonic acid, which serves to build up the structure of the plant, and the latter in its turn gives out oxygen to supply the consumption of animals.

Every day—in the middle of the day, in winter, in the summer, early in the morning, or in the evening—gymnastic training on the system of the Swedish anatomist Ling or of the German Turners would form a portion of the curriculum, for which convenient apparatus would be provided.

Biography should form an important feature in the course of reading, its subjects being arranged in groups; and the true glory of a Washington, a Bentham, a Stevenson, a Morse, and a Cobden distinguished from the false glare and tinsel of a Louis XIV. and a Marlborough.

Music, both vocal and instrumental, would be taught to all, but only those more gifted by nature would be educated to perform solo. Nearly all persons can be trained to sing part-music pleasantly and intelligently, and to perform moderately on some instrument. The cultivation of the musical faculties harmonizes the mind, and affords a never-failing source of solace and recreation. The attempt to convert all persons into solo performers, and the hypocritical applause with which their discordant notes are indiscriminately greeted, deprives society of the pleasures which part-music well performed would afford, by encouraging all to attempt what they are pretty sure to do badly, to the exclusion of what they would be equally likely to do well.

We have reserved for the last, to enumerate what is, perhaps, the most important of all the subjects of instruction.

To ALL children, so soon as they can be promoted from the *kinder garten*—perhaps even to the higher grades therein—instruction in the conditions of human well-being, and in the phenomena and arrangements of social life should be given, and should be continued throughout their school career.

What! teach political economy to children? Even so. It will be conceded, that to teach the future laborers the laws by which the wages of their labor will be regulated, how high wages may be secured and low wages prevented—to teach the future capitalists the laws by which their profits will be deter-

mined, how large profits may be secured, and loss,
failure, crises, and panics avoided—must be a desirable, if it be a practicable thing.   Is it practicable?
The experience of twenty years has proved that it is.
The experiment has been tried by Mr. Wm. Ellis, the
wise and noble founder of the Birkbeck schools of
London, England, who not only devoted his surplus
means to the endowment of true schools, but gave
also his time to instruct in the principles of the science of human well-being—alike the poor children
by whom his schools were attended and the children
of the Queen of England.   He also instructed and
trained a corps of teachers, professional and volun-
teer, and by one of the latter a class was conducted in
the winter of 1867, '68 at the Normal School of this
city of some 35 to 40 teachers engaged in the practical work of teaching in our common schools, who,
under his guidance, became, after a short course of
some twenty or more lessons, enthusiastic advocates
for the introduction of this study into the schools;
for not only does it teach the conditions of industrial
success, but it is also a science of morals and of ethics
far more worthy of the attention it has never yet received in this or, indeed, in any country, than that
which is given to what goes under the name of moral
teaching and training.   It is by gradual steps—by
the employment of the Socratic method of instruction
—with a rare use of text-books, that the most intri-
cate problems of this science can be unfolded to pupils with such effect that a child of fourteen or fifteen
years of age, who shall have passed through a course
of four or five years' instruction, would put to the
blush, with few exceptions, alike the members of both

houses of the United States Congress and of the British Parliament.

A museum and a library would be necessary ad-
juncts to such a school as we have described. It
would need but a few seasons to get together in the
various excursions taken by pupils and teachers,
quite a collection of botanical, entomological, and geo-
logical specimens. These would serve as objects for
illustrating the teacher's lessons, and for examination
by the pupils. The drying, preservation, and arrangement of plants, animals, and minerals, in which the
pupils would assist, would serve to impart to them a
skill and dexterity, which they would know how to
value, and would be eager to acquire, and, together
with their frequent visits to the museum, would serve
to cultivate a love of nature and devotion to the study
of her works.

The library, besides containing treatises on science
and for reference, would be filled with books of trav-
els, and the nobler English and foreign classics; the
books would be loaned to the pupils as in ordinary
circulating libraries, and a pleasant reading - room
would be furnished with the better class of periodi-
cals and newspapers.

To be deprived for a time of the right to visit the
museum or reading - room, or to borrow books from
the library, would be one of the severest punishments
known in the school.

It is hardly necessary to say that the selection of
the principal of such a school as we have indicated
is among the most difficult problems of its establish-
ment. His qualifications should be as near the perfection of manhood as can possibly be found.   Invited

by a large and generous salary (to be dependent, beyond a stated sum, on the number of the pupils), it is to be hoped such a teacher could be found.

Such a principal, after a fixed period of probation, should not be removable except on a very large vote of the proprietors of the school to that effect, but his office should be vacated on his attaining the age of 60 or 65 years. The selection of teachers to assist him in his duties should be left to himself. The remuneration of the assistant teachers should also be large, and should be such as not only to enable them to live in comfort, but to make ample provision for their future when the age of labor shall have passed.

The chief position in society should be assured to the principal and his assistants by the proprietors of the school.

The visits of the former to the houses of the latter should be regarded as an honor, the greatest respect and deference should be paid to them, and the pupils should be taught to look upon them with love and respect next only to that they pay their parents.

The best investment a parent can make of his wealth is in the proper education of his children. Life is not merely to be born, to grow, to eat, to drink, and breathe. Noise is not music. Life is such as we take it and make it, or rather as it is taken hold of and made for us by those to whom the care of our youthful days is intrusted.

Let us endeavor to picture to ourselves the being likely to be produced by a system of teaching and training, continued for successive generations, such as we have indicated above. Let us imagine the full development of the most complex of nature's organ-

isms—a part of the one living organism of the Uni
verse, the latest product of her laboratory; considered, as a part of the great Cosmos, the most perfect,
yet but an integer in the whole; the ultimate development of nature's chemistry, yet forming an atom
of her living unity; combining and possessing the
widest relationships, even embracing therein the entire volume of that nature whose true relationships
comprise all knowledge, truly "the noblest study of
mankind." Let us try and draw the picture of the
developed man!

Robust and supple of limb, symmetrical of shape,
his muscles swelling beneath their healthy development; with head erect, conscious of his strength and
skill, which he puts forth for the protection of the
weak, and for the purpose of drawing from nature
her bounteous stores; free from sickness or disease,
in harmony with nature, at peace with his fellow-men,
possessing a competent knowledge of nature's laws,
and guiding his conduct to be in accord therewith,
"sitting beneath his own vine and fig-tree," "blessed
in all the works of his hands," and diffusing blessings
and happiness around. Such is the picture of THE
HEALTHY MIND IN A HEALTHY FRAME, which it is in
man's power to procreate and rear!

APPENDIX.

4

APPENDIX.

Department of Public Instruction,
Corner of Grand and Elm Streets,
New York, June 5th, 1869.

To Magnus Gross, Esq.,

*Chairman of the "Executive Committee for the Care, Government
and Management of the College of the City of New York:"*

Dear Sir,—I have observed with surprise, and with a
sense of deep regret, that the proposition is entertained
by a large number of the Trustees of filling the chair of
Latin and Greek, now vacant, and even of establishing
separate chairs for each, at the College of the City of
New York; involving, with the necessary tutors, an out-
lay of not less than $20,000 per annum. The subject in
all its bearings is one of too vast importance to be treated in the ordinary method of discussion by the Committee, and I therefore beg leave to place my views in
writing, to insure their receiving more matured consideration than oral observations could secure.

I pass over the question (on which considerable difference of opinion exists) as to the propriety of sustain-
ing at all, at the enforced expense of the public, an educational institution to supply the needs which the College of the City of New York is intended to meet. The
College exists by law; we are its guardians, and the only
question we have to consider is, how most efficiently and
most economically to secure the attainment of the ends
desired by the Legislature.

These ends we shall no doubt all agree to be—first:
that any of the youth of this city possessed of special
talents, but lacking means for their cultivation, may
have placed within their reach an education the best
possible for the development of their powers for the

benefit of themselves and of the community; and, second, to provide for the comparatively well-to-do the means of pursuing useful studies in compensation for compelling them to provide for the instruction of their less fortunate citizens.

As it is self-evident that whatever course of studies will tend to secure the first of these ends will tend also to secure the second and less important, we are spared the necessity of a two-fold investigation.

A very few statistics suffice to show that neither of these ends has been hitherto attained by the College of the City of New York.

It is immaterial what year we select for examination, the numbers which follow will be found to bear about the same relative proportions in every year. I quote from the Trustees' Report for 1866 merely because it is the latest document at hand which furnishes the numbers in the different classes and of the graduates; from this report I find, that while there were three hundred and eighty-one students in the introductory class, only twenty-five graduated in that year. The number of graduates in 1867 was thirty, and twenty-nine in July, 1868. Of the three hundred and eighty-one who composed the introductory class in 1866, one hundred and fifty-one left the College during the year, and doubtless the two hundred and thirty who remained will have dwindled to about twenty-five or thirty by the year 1871.

Without doubt some proportion of the three hundred and eighty-one leave the College because of the necessity they are under of obtaining, by their labor, the means of subsistence; but when it is remembered that these three hundred and eighty-one are the *picked youth from the many thousands attending the public schools,* and when the sacrifices and privations which men and youth imbued with a love of learning will make and undergo for the acquirement of knowledge are borne in mind, we must look to something in the constitution of the College itself to account for this result. In short, we can but come to the conclusion that the main cause of this falling off is to be found in the feeling which grows upon the pupils and their guardians, of the comparative uselessness of the studies to which they are consigned.

Let us examine the course of studies, as given from pages 8 to 14 of the Report of the Board of Trustees for the year 1866, or from pages 24 to 28 of the Manual of the College.

The first observation which must strike the mind of every thinker is the fact that the primary analysis—the main classification which has been adopted of studies which ought to be framed to fit the students for " complete living "—is one of " words," *i. e.*, the tools of knowledge, instead of knowledge itself. Or in the words of the Report : " There are two courses of studies—ancient and modern—differing only in the languages studied."

On examining the course for the introductory and freshman classes, a feeling of astonishment must fill the mind at the marked want of wisdom by which it was dictated, but which at the same time affords a sufficient explanation for the abandonment of the College by its students.

Even if " *words* " ought to be the real object of education, it would be supposed that English words would be more useful to a people whose mother-tongue is English, than the words of any other language; yet the students of the introductory and freshman classes of the ancient course receive instruction *five hours a week through both terms in Latin and Greek,* and *one lesson per week during one term in the English language.* The students of the modern course substitute for Latin and Greek the French and Spanish languages.

I purposely abstain from saying any thing as to the method of instruction, which is the converse of that adopted by nature, and as a consequence signally fails. This has been so forcibly put by President Barnard, of Columbia College, that I need only refer the members of our Committee to his essay on "Early Mental Training, and the Studies best fitted for it."

What steps are taken to familiarize the students of,
say the freshman class, with that great nature of which
they form a part?   What, for instance, do they learn of
the structure of their own bodies, and of the means of
preserving health?   *One lesson a week* is given on Physiology and Hygiene, and that is all!   The fear of making
this letter too long compels me merely to refer the Committee to pages 40 to 42 of Mr. Herbert Spencer's chapter on "What Knowledge is of Most Worth," in his
work on Education, in farther illustration of this subject, instead of making extracts from it as I would otherwise like to do.

Attention, it is true, is paid throughout the college
course to mathematical studies, yet very little to their
practical application; while to Chemistry, the parent of
modern physics, the manual (which is our guide) proscribes two lessons per week to the introductory class,
and to the freshman, sophomore, and junior classes absolutely *none at all!*   Mining, Mechanical Engineering,
Architecture, Theoretical Agriculture, Biology, and Botany are utterly ignored; and no branch of Zoology is
even mentioned in the curriculum.   We next come to
a science more important, because universal in its application and in its need than any other, viz. : The Science
of Human Well-being, commonly called Political or Social Economy.   Here, too, like exclusion! except that
in the sophomore class, for one term, one hour per week
is given to it.   That is to say, a people who are to live
by labor are left by the guardians of their education in
ignorance of the laws by which the reward for that labor
must be regulated; they who are to administer capital
are to be left to blind chance whether to act in accordance with those laws of nature which determine its increase, or ignorantly to violate them!

Restrained again from quotation by the fear of wearying the Committee, permit me to refer them to the lec ture of Dr. Hodgson, delivered at the Royal Institution of Great Britain, on "The Importance of the Study of Economic Science," which will be found in the work of Professor Youmans, on "The Culture demanded by Modern Life."

I confess to a feeling of deep discouragement at the perusal of such a record as that presented by the course of studies at the College of the City of New York, especially when I find that this is the state of things a large number of the Trustees seem desirous of perpetuating. My views on this subject are confirmed by the following remarks found in President Barnard's Essay on "Early Mental Training, and the Studies best fitted for it."

"Whatever may be the value of the study of the classics in a subjective point of view, *nothing could possibly more thoroughly unfit a man for any immediate usefulness* in this matter-of-fact world, or make him *more completely a stranger in his own home*, than the purely classical education which used recently to be given, and which, with some slight improvement, is believed to be still given by the universities of England. This proposition is very happily enforced by a British writer, whose strictures on the system appeared in the London *Times* some twelve or thirteen years ago.

"Common things are quite as much neglected and despised in the education of the rich as in that of the poor. It is wonderful *how little a young gentleman may know when he has taken his university degrees, especially if he has been industrious, and has stuck to his studies*. He may really *spend a long time in looking for somebody more ignorant than himself*. If he talks with the driver of the stage-coach that lands him at his father's door, he finds he knows nothing of horses. If he falls into conversation with a gardener, he knows nothing of plants or flowers. If he walks into the fields, he does not know the difference between barley, rye, and wheat; between rape and turnips; between natural and artificial grass. If he goes into a carpenter's yard, he does not know one wood from another. If he comes across an attorney, he has no idea of the difference between common and statute law, and is wholly in the dark as to those securities of personal and political liberty on which we pride ourselves. If he talks with a country magistrate, he finds his only idea of the office is that the gentleman is a sort of English Sheik, as the Mayor of the neighboring borough is a sort of Cadi. If he strolls into any workshop or place of manufacture, it is always to find his level, and that a level far below the present company. If he dines out, and as a youth of proved talents and perhaps university honors is expected to be literary, his literature is confined to a few popular novels—the novels of the last century, or even of the last generation—history and poetry having been almost studiously omitted in his education. *The girl who has never stirred from home, and whose education has been economized, not to say neglected, in order to send her own brother to college,* knows vastly more of those things than he does. The same exposure awaits him wherever he goes, and whenever he has the audacity to open his mouth. *At sea he is a landlubber; in the country a cockney; in town a greenhorn; in science an ignoramus; in business a simpleton; in pleasure a milksop*—everywhere out of his element, everywhere at sea, in the clouds, adrift, or by whatever word *utter ignorance* and *incapacity* are to be described. In society and in the work of life, he finds himself beaten by the youth whom at college he despised as frivolous or abhorred as profligate."

Take the preparation of our youth for their duties as citizens. Here, again, a knowledge of political and social economy is indispensable. We have seen the attention it receives; and while two lessons a week for one hour, and that only to the senior class in its last term, are given to American citizens on the Constitution of the United States and on International Law, *none whatever is given on the science of Government throughout the entire course of five years!*

I might go through the whole course of studies with similar results. Here and there, in this or that class, a small amount of attention is given to some of the sciences omitted in the other classes; but the entire record is one of the most disheartening character.

Words! words! engross almost exclusively the attention of the students from the hour they enter the College until they leave it; and it is not to the five-and-twenty graduates the palm of useful industry should be awarded, but to the many who, in discouragement, abandon a course which tends to *unfit* them for the great battle of life!

What, then, are the reasons generally assigned for this perverse conventionalism of devoting the time of youth to the acquirement of dead words, to the unavoidable exclusion of nearly every thing that is of value? First, we are told that we can not understand the English language without a knowledge of Latin, from which it is derived. The inaccuracy of this pretension is at once made manifest by reference to Webster, where he states:

"That English is composed of—

"*First.* Saxon and Danish words of Teutonic and Gothic origin.

"*Second.* British or Welsh, Cornish and Amoric, which may be considered as of Celtic origin.

"*Third.* Norman, a mixture of French and Gothic.

"*Fourth.* Latin, a language formed on the Celtic and Teutonic.

"*Fifth.* French, chiefly Latin corrupted, but with a mixture of Celtic.

"*Sixth.* Greek formed on the Celtic and Teutonic, with some Coptic.

"*Seventh.* A few words directly from the Italian, Spanish, German, and other languages of the Continent.

"*Eighth.* A few foreign words, introduced by commerce, or by political and literary intercourse.

"Of these, *the Saxon words constitute our mother-tongue*, being words which our ancestors brought with them from Asia.

"The Danish and Welsh also are primitive words, and may be considered as a part of our vernacular language. They are of equal antiquity with the Chaldee and Syriac."

But even were it true that our language was derived from the Latin, wherein lies the difficulty in the way of the teacher explaining to his pupils the meanings of the parts of English words which are of Latin origin, without the necessity of the pupil's acquiring the same knowledge by the roundabout process of learning one thousand words he will never need, for one that may at some time be to him of some service as a mnemonic?

Driven from this position, the advocates of "*classical*" studies tell us that the study of Latin and Greek serves as a training for the intellect. Unquestionably the exercise of the faculties of the mind serves to develop the faculties so exercised; yet if this were the object to be attained, Hebrew, nay, Chinese, would be preferable to Latin; but SCIENCE develops the same faculties, and far more efficiently. The facts of science to be stored up in the mind are so infinite in number and magnitude that no man, however gifted, could ever hope to master them all, though he were to live a thousand years. But their arrangement in scientific order not only develops the analytical powers of the mind, but exercises the memory in a method infinitely more useful and powerful than the study of any language. Finally we are told classical studies develop the taste. If then to this the advocates of such studies are driven, its mere announcement must

suffice to banish Latin and Greek from all schools sup-
ported by taxation; for however essential it may be to
provide the means of the best possible instruction, it is
as absolutely out of the sphere of the Trustees of Public
Moneys to provide, at the public expense, so *mere a lux-
ury* as on this hypothesis Latin and Greek must be, as
it would be to provide the public with costly jewels!
But even for the cultivation and development of art and
taste, SCIENCE is the true curriculum!

He who is ignorant of anatomy can not appreciate
either sculpture or painting! A knowledge of optics, of
botany and of natural history, are necessary, equally to
the artist or to the connoisseur; a knowledge of acous-
tics to the musician and musical critic. "No artist,"
says Mr. Spencer, "can produce a healthful work of
whatever kind without he understands the laws of the
phenomena he represents; he must also understand how
the minds of the spectator or listener will be affected by
his work—a question of psychology." The spectator or
listener must equally be acquainted with the laws of such
phenomena, or he fails to attain to the highest appreciation.

I now come to the last and most serious aspect of
this question, and I fearlessly assert that classical studies have a most pernicious influence upon the morals and
character of their votaries.

It should not be forgotten that Greeks and Romans
alike lived by slavery (which is robbery), by rapine, and
by plunder; yet we, born into a Christian community
which lives by honest labor, propose to impregnate the
impressionable minds of youth with the morals and literature of nations of robbers!

This letter has already extended to so great a length
that I am compelled to abstain from making extracts
from the works of the greatest thinkers, which I had desired: and I can now but cite them in support, more or
less pronounced, of the views above put forward, viz.:
President Barnard, of Columbia College, who with rare

honesty and boldness has spoken loudly against the conventional folly of classical studies; Professor Newman, himself Professor of Latin at the University of London, England; Professors Tindall, Henfry, Huxley, Forbes, Pajet, Whewell, Faraday, Liebig, Draper, De Morgan, Lindley, Youmans, Drs. Hodgson, Carpenter, Hooker, Acland, Sir John Herschell, Sir Charles Lyell, Dr. Seguin, and, rising above them all in *educational science*, *Bastiat* and *Herbert Spencer*. To a modified extent, the name of Mr. John Stuart Mill may be quoted—for he loudly advocates science for all—science, which is unavoidably excluded by the introduction of, or at least the prominence given to, Latin and Greek in our College. Mr. Mill, it is true also, advocates classical studies, but for certain special classes which exist in England who have no regular occupations in life.

Neither is it without importance as a guide to ourselves to observe that in the very best school in this country—a school perhaps not surpassed by any in the world, viz., the Military Academy at West Point—neither Latin nor Greek studies are permitted.

If now, in any career whatever, any use could be found for Latin, it must be in that of the professional soldier, to whom, if to any one, the language and literature of the most military people the world has ever seen, should be of some service. But no! the wise men who framed the curriculum of West Point, though they knew that the study of the campaigns of the Romans would be serviceable to their students, provided for their study, *not* by the roundabout method of first learning a language which could never be of any other use, but by the direct method of the study of those campaigns! Are the pupils of West Point generally found deficient in intellect? Is not, on the contrary, the fact of having graduated at that school a passport to the *highest scientific* and *practical* employment?

Our duty to the people is clear; let us neither waste the precious time of our youth on worse than useless studies, nor the money of the citizens on worse than use-less expenditure.

I do earnestly hope that our Committee will give to my observations their most serious deliberation. Let us come to no hasty conclusion on this subject : accustomed as we have been to hear constantly repeated such conventional phrases as that " Latin and Greek are essential to the education of a gentleman ;" that " classical studies are indispensable to a liberal education ;" to hear applauded to the echo orators who have introduced into their speeches quotations of bad Latin or worse Greek by audiences of whom not one in one thousand understand what was said. We have been apt to receive such phrases as embodying truths, without ever examining their foundations. I respectfully urge the Committee to consider well before they act, to study the reasons assigned by the great thinkers I have named for condemning, as, humbly following in their wake, I venture to condemn, as worse than mere waste of time, the years devoted to Latin and Greek studies.

Let us endeavor to make the College of this city worthy of the city and of the state; let us cast aside the trammels of mediæval ignorance, and supply to the pupils of the College " the culture demanded by modern life." Let us in this, the first important matter which has come before our Committee, act in harmony and without prejudice, for the welfare of the College and " for the advancement of learning," and so prove ourselves worthy of the sacred trust we have assumed.

I am, dear sir, very truly yours,

NATHANIEL SANDS,

Member of " The Executive Committee for the Care, Government, and Management of the College of the City of New York."

The Philosophy of Teaching.

THE TEACHER,

THE PUPIL, THE SCHOOL.

By NATHANIEL SANDS.

8vo, Cloth, $1 00.

An interesting and valuable work, in which the science of teaching is treated in a philosophical and practical manner, and a sketch is given of a school to be established on the principles developed in his pages. Mr. Sands takes the view that education, mental and physical, is but the absorption of surrounding elements into the mind and body—an arrangement and assimilation of materials so as to incorporate them into the being to whose nourishment they are applied, just as the tree or plant assimilates to its growth and subsistence the materials which it draws from the air and the soil ; and his theory of teaching is based on these truths.—*N. Y. Times.*

He advocates a radical change in the system of teaching youth. He proposes a school where pupils shall be taught by illustrations from nature as well as from books ; where the museum, chemical laboratory, and workshop shall find a place ; where, in short, the mind of the learner shall not be forced, but shall have just the kind of food suitable for its age and development.—*N. Y. World.*

Much has been written upon education—much that is both wise and thoughtful, and much that has been but sound. Among the most thoughtful and suggestive recent writings is an unpretentious work bearing the title of "The Teacher, the Pupil, the School," by Mr. Nathaniel Sands. Small as it is, it contains more ideas than many bulky volumes.—*N. Y. Tribune.*

The question with which he mainly concerns himself is whether Latin and Greek, and certain other branches, shall be taught to the exclusion of more practical studies. He thinks that what is commonly known as the "culture demanded by modern life"—chemistry, mining, anatomy, natural history, political and social economy, the science of government, etc.—should take the place now usurped by classical studies. Mr. Sands believes in making no compromise between the useful sciences and the classics. He condemns "as worse than mere waste of time the years devoted to Greek and Latin," and would bar them out altogether.—*Journal of Commerce.*

Mr. Sands, who has just been appointed one of the new Board of Education, has long been known as an advanced thinker on the subject he is now called upon to deal with. He has published a pamphlet on the Philosophy of Education.—*N. Y. Sun.*

We have in this compact and unpretentious treatise a great deal of pith and acumen, brought to bear upon a most important subject—that of educational first principles. Mr. Sands has gone to the base of human teaching, discarding pretentious themes, in order to illustrate the simpler beauty of that eductive and inductive co-relationship which, beginning at the mother's breast, proceeds through all the quiet processes of mental development in infancy, childhood, and maturity.—*N. Y. Dispatch.*

His hints may well arrest the attention of thoughtful men.—*N. Y. Tribune.*

We commend it to the thoughtful consideration of all, but especially of our public men. * * * Commissioners of Schools and others charged with youthful training may advantageously consider the reflections.—*N. Y. Evening Post.*

HARPER & BROTHERS, Publishers,

Franklin Square, New York.

☞ Harper & Brothers *will send the above work by mail, postage prepaid, to any part of the United States, on receipt of* $1 00.

Works on Education

PUBLISHED BY

HARPER & BROTHERS, New York.

☞ Harper & Brothers *will send any of the following books by mail, postage prepaid, to any part of the United States, on receipt of the price.*

☞ Harper's Catalogue *and* Trade-List *will be sent by mail on receipt of Five Cents, or they may be obtained gratuitously on application to the Publishers personally.*

RANDALL'S POPULAR EDUCATION. First Principles of Popular Education and Public Instruction. By S. S. Randall, Superintendent of Public Schools of the City of New York. 12mo, Cloth, $1 50.

SANDS'S PHILOSOPHY OF TEACHING. The Teacher, the Pupil, the School. By Nathaniel Sands. 8vo, Cloth.

BURTON'S OBSERVING FACULTIES. The Culture of the Observing Faculties in the Family and the School; or, Things about Home, and how to make them Instructive to the Young. By Warren Burton, Author of "The District School as it was," "Helps to Education," &c. 16mo, Cloth, 75 cents.

CALKINS'S PRIMARY OBJECT LESSONS. Primary Object Lessons for a Graduated Course of Development. A Manual for Teachers and Parents, with Lessons for the Proper Training of the Faculties of the Children. By N. A. Calkins. Illustrations. 12mo, Cloth, $1 50.

WILLSON'S OBJECT LESSONS. A Manual of Information and Suggestions for Object Lessons, in a Course of Elementary Instruction. Adapted to the Use of the School and Family Charts, and other Aids in Teaching. By Marcius Willson. 12mo, Cloth, $1 50.

ABBOTT'S TEACHER. Moral Influences Employed in the Instruction and Government of the Young. By Jacob Abbott. With Engravings. 12mo, Cloth, $1 75.

BOESÉ'S EDUCATION IN NEW YORK CITY.
Public Education in the City of New York : its History, Condition, and Statistics.   An Official Report to the Board of Education.   By THOMAS BOESÉ, Clerk of the Board.   With Illustrations.   8vo, Cloth, $1 50.

BEECHER'S TRAINING OF CHILDREN.   The
Religious Training of Children in the Family, the School, and the Church.   By CATHARINE E. BEECHER.   12mo, Cloth, $1 75.

EDGEWORTH'S PRACTICAL EDUCATION.   A
Treatise on Practical Education.   By RICHARD LOVELL EDGEWORTH and MARIA EDGEWORTH.   Engravings.   12mo, Cloth, $1 50.

SIR WILLIAM HAMILTON'S ESSAYS.   Discussions on Philosophy and Literature, Education and University Reform.   Chiefly from the Edinburgh Review.   Corrected, Vindicated, and Enlarged, in Notes and Appendices.   By Sir WILLIAM HAMILTON, Bart.   With an Introductory Essay, by Rev. ROBERT TURNBULL, D.D.   8vo, Cloth, $3 00.

DR. OLIN'S COLLEGE ADDRESSES.   College Life :
its Theory and Practice.   By Rev. STEPHEN OLIN, D.D., LL.D., late President of the Wesleyan University.   12mo, Cloth, $1 50.

POTTER & EMERSON'S MANUAL.   The School
and the Schoolmaster.   A Manual for the Use of Teachers, Employers, Trustees, Inspectors, &c., &c.   In Two Parts.   Part I. By Rt. Rev. ALONZO POTTER, D.D.   Part II. By GEORGE B. EMERSON, A.M., of Massachusetts.   Part I. The School ; its Objects, Relations, and Uses.   With a Sketch of the Education most needed in the United States, the present State of Common Schools, the best Means of Improving them, and the consequent Duties of Parents, Trustees, Inspectors, &c.   Part II. The proper Character, Studies, and Duties of the Teacher, with the best Methods for the Government and Instruction for the Common Schools, and the Principles on which School-Houses should be Built, Arranged, Warmed, and Ventilated.   Engravings.   12mo, Cloth, $1 50.

EVERETT ON PRACTICAL EDUCATION.   Importance of Practical Education and Useful Knowledge : being a Selection from the Orations and Discourses of EDWARD EVERETT, President of Harvard University.   12mo, Cloth, $1 50.